RITE OF BAPTISM

FOR ONE CHILD
and
FOR SEVERAL CHILDREN

according to texts approved by
the National Conference of Bishops of the United States
and confirmed by the Apostolic See

THE LITURGICAL PRESS
Collegeville, Minnesota

www.litpress.org

ISBN 0-8146-2923-7

HOLY BAPTISM

Baptism is our birth as Christians, our birth as "other Christs." Through many centuries Christians loved to view the baptismal font as the womb of holy Mother Church; for at the font her children come forth alive with a new and higher life—that of God Himself.

This second birth into God's own family at the sacred font is the source of new and wonderful privileges. The first of the baptismal graces which needs emphasis in twenty-first-century United States is that of our incorporation into Christ, the face of the Mystical Body. Baptism makes us members of Christ: "We were all baptized into one Body . . . you are the Body of Christ and individually parts of it" (1 Cor 12:13, 27). Our head is Christ, and consequently the thoughts which fill our minds must be His thoughts: "We have the mind of Christ" (1 Cor 2:16). As in a body many cells share the same dignity, so the many individuals who form Christ's Body all share the same godlike dignity; there is then no place for mutual indignities or antagonisms; fraternal charity must reign supreme. Because Baptism has made us all one in Christ, the efforts of each are to the advantage of all, the suffering of one brings tears to many, a single song of praise gladdens countless hearts.

Baptism, secondly, makes us the dwelling-place of the most Blessed Trinity, makes each of us a holy temple, for "holy is the temple of God, and this temple you are" (1 Cor 3:17). God's active, energizing presence in the baptized soul transforms it into a creature most pleasing to Himself. Too frequently we may have limited our attentions to the negative aspect of holy Baptism, that is its power to remit sin and to cleanse away all guilt. More marvelous is its fulfillment of Jesus' last prayer: "If any one love me, he will keep my word, and my Father will love him, and *we will come to him and will make our abode with him*" (John 14:23). And where Father and Son are, their Spirit must of necessity be: "Do you not know that the Spirit of God dwells in you?" (1 Cor 3:16). As we become conscious of this unspeakable gift our hearts spontaneously welcome the command: "Glorify and bear God in your body" (1 Cor 6:20).

Though Baptism confers such great gifts, it is not a final stage in God's generosity toward us—it is only a beginning. Baptism plants the seed, the remaining sacraments bring it to harvest. All the sacraments are directed toward the Holy Eucharist, particularly Baptism. Baptism gives me the right to receive the Holy Eucharist while the Holy Eucharist preserves and makes fruitful my baptismal privileges. Baptism, by making me share in the priesthood of Christ through the "character" it imprints, enables me to share in the offering of the one only Sacrifice; by offering this Sacrifice with Christ I again renew my baptismal descent with Christ into death in order to raise again with Him in newness of life. Baptism makes me a cell in Christ's Body, the Eucharist nourishes that cell, makes it healthy, makes it function in a loving, sacrificial spirit of unity with countless other cells, makes it ever a more fitting dwelling for the triune God.

Baptism is our birth as Christians. A little reflection, and this age-old truth becomes fresh and dynamic. Its power produced the Age of Martyrs and the glories of patristic Christianity. If we but give holy Baptism the thought and attention it deserves, its power will vitalize and transform our weak devotions into a spirituality strong with the strength of Christ our Head and holy with the holiness of the indwelling Trinity. Its power will make us pleasing and acceptable to the eternal Father, for through it we have been enabled to offer the perfect Sacrifice in and through it we have been enabled to offer the perfect Sacrifice in and through His Son Christ Jesus. Truly, holy Baptism is a great sacrament, making us Christians, making us "a kingdom of priests, a holy people" (1 Pet 2:9).

RITE OF BAPTISM
FOR ONE CHILD

RECEPTION OF THE CHILD

If possible, baptism should take place on Sunday, the day on which the Church celebrates the paschal mystery. It should be conferred in a communal celebration in the presence of the faithful, or at least of relatives, friends, and neighbors, who are all to take an active part in the rite.

It is the role of the father and mother, accompanied by the godparents, to present the child to the Church for baptism.

The people may sing a psalm or hymn suitable for the occasion. Meanwhile the celebrating priest or deacon, vested in alb or surplice, with a stole (with or without a cope) of festive color, and accompanied by the ministers goes to the entrance of the church or to that part of the church where the parents and godparents are waiting with the child.

The celebrant greets all present, and especially the parents and godparents, reminding them briefly of the joy with which the parents welcomed this child as a gift from God, the source of life, who now wishes to bestow his own life on this little one.

First the celebrant questions the parents:

Celebrant:

What name do you give your child? (or: **have you given?**)

Parents:

N.

Celebrant:

What do you ask of God's Church for N.?

Parents:

Baptism.

The celebrant may choose other words for this dialogue.

The first reply may be given by someone other than the parents if local custom gives him the right to name the child.

In the second response the parents may use other words, e.g., faith or the grace of Christ or entrance into the Church or eternal life.

The celebrant speaks to the parents in these or similar words:

You have asked to have your child baptized. In doing so you are accepting the responsibility of training him (her) in the practice of the faith. It will be your duty to bring him (her) up to keep God's commandments as Christ taught us, by loving God and our neighbor. Do you clearly understand what you are undertaking?

Parents:

We do.

Then the celebrant turns to the godparents and addresses them in these or similar words:

Are you ready to help the parents of this child in their duty as Christian parents?

Godparents:

We are.

The celebrant continues:

N., the Christian community welcomes you with great joy. In its name I claim you for Christ our Savior by the sign of his cross. I now trace the cross on your forehead, and invite your parents (and godparents) to do the same.

He signs the child on the forehead, in silence. Then he invites the parents and (if it seems appropriate) the godparents to do the same.

The celebrant invites the parents, godparents, and the others to take part in the liturgy of the word. If circumstances permit, there is a procession to the place where this will be celebrated, during which a song is sung, e.g., Psalm 84:7, 8, 9ab:

Will you not give us life;
and shall not your people rejoice in you?
Show us, O Lord, your kindness,
and grant us your salvation.
I will hear what God proclaims;
the Lord—for he proclaims peace to his people.

LITURGY OF THE WORD

SCRIPTURAL READINGS AND HOMILY

> One or even two gospel passages are read, during which all may sit if convenient.

Matthew 28:18-20

✢ A reading from the holy Gospel according to Matthew

Go, therefore, and make disciples of all nations, baptizing them in the name of the Father, and of the Son, and of the Holy Spirit.

Jesus said to the Eleven disciples:
"All power in heaven and on earth has been given to me.
Go, therefore, and make disciples of all nations,
   baptizing them in the name of the Father,
   and of the Son, and of the Holy Spirit,
   teaching them to observe all that I have commanded you.
And behold, I am with you always, until the end of the age."

The Gospel of the Lord.

> Alternate choices of readings, together with responsorial psalms and verses before the gospel, are given on pages 39–56.

> After the reading, the celebrant gives a short homily, explaining to those present the significance of what has been read. His purpose will be to lead them to a deeper understanding of the mystery of baptism and to encourage the parents and godparents to a ready acceptance of the responsibilities which arise from the sacrament.

> After the homily, or in the course of or after the litany, it is desirable to have a period of silence while all pray at the invitation of the celebrant.

GENERAL INTERCESSIONS

> Then the general intercessions are said:

> Celebrant:

My dear brothers and sisters,* let us ask our Lord Jesus Christ to look lovingly on this child who is to be baptized, on his (her) parents and godparents, and on all the baptized.

> *At the discretion of the priest, other words which seem more suitable under the circumstances, such as **friends, dearly beloved, brethren,** may be used. This also applies to parallel instances in the liturgy.

Leader:

By the mystery of your death and resurrection, bathe this child in light, give him (her) the new life of baptism and welcome him (her) into your holy Church.

All:

Lord, hear our prayer.

Leader:

Through baptism and confirmation, make him (her) your faithful follower and a witness to your gospel.

All:

Lord, hear our prayer.

Leader:

Lead him (her) by a holy life to the joys of God's kingdom.

All:

Lord, hear our prayer.

Leader:

Make the lives of his (her) parents and godparents examples of faith to inspire this child.

All:

Lord, hear our prayer.

Leader:

Keep his (her) family always in your love.

All:

Lord, hear our prayer.

Leader:

Renew the grace of our baptism in each one of us.

All:

Lord, hear our prayer.

The celebrant next invites all present to invoke the saints.

Holy Mary, Mother of God,   **pray for us.**
Saint John the Baptist,   **pray for us.**
Saint Joseph,   **pray for us.**
Saint Peter and Saint Paul,   **pray for us.**

The names of other saints may be added, especially the patrons of the child to be baptized, and of the church or locality. The litany concludes:

All holy men and women, **pray for us.**

PRAYER OF EXORCISM AND ANOINTING BEFORE BAPTISM

After the invocation, the celebrant says:

Almighty and ever-living God, you sent your only Son into the world to cast out the power of Satan, spirit of evil, to rescue man from the kingdom of darkness, and bring him into the splendor of your kingdom of light. We pray for this child: set him (her) free from original sin, make him (her) a temple of your glory, and send your Holy Spirit to dwell with him (her). (We ask this) through Christ our Lord.

All:

Amen.

The celebrant continues:

We anoint you with the oil of salvation in the name of Christ our Savior; may he strengthen you with his power, who lives and reigns for ever and ever.

All:

Amen.

He anoints the child on the breast with the oil of catechumens.

If, for serious reasons, the conference of bishops so decides, the anointing before baptism may be omitted. [In the United States, it may be omitted only when the minister of baptism judges the omission to be pastorally necessary or desirable.] In that case the celebrant says:

May you have strength in the power of Christ our Savior, who lives and reigns for ever and ever.

All:

Amen.

And immediately he lays his hand on the child in silence.

Then they go to the baptistery, or to the sanctuary when baptism is celebrated there on occasion.

CELEBRATION OF THE SACRAMENT

> When they come to the font, the celebrant briefly reminds the congregation of the wonderful work of God whose plan it is to sanctify man, body and soul, through water. He may use these or similar words:

A My dear brothers and sisters, we now ask God to give this child new life in abundance through water and the Holy Spirit.

or:

B My dear brothers and sisters, God uses the sacrament of water to give his divine life to those who believe in him. Let us turn to him, and ask him to pour his gift of life from this font on this child he has chosen.

BLESSING AND INVOCATION OF GOD OVER BAPTISMAL WATER

> Then, turning to the font, he says the following blessing (outside the Easter season):

Father, you give us grace through sacramental signs, which tell us of the wonders of your unseen power.

In baptism we use your gift of water, which you have made a rich symbol of the grace you give us in this sacrament.

At the very dawn of creation your Spirit breathed on the waters, making them the wellspring of all holiness.

The waters of the great flood you made a sign of the waters of baptism, that make an end of sin and a new beginning of goodness.

Through the waters of the Red Sea you led Israel out of slavery, to be an image of God's holy people, set free from sin by baptism.

In the waters of the Jordan your Son was baptized by John and anointed with the Spirit.

Your Son willed that water and blood should flow from his side as he hung upon the cross.

After his resurrection he told his disciples: "Go out and teach all nations, baptizing them in the name of the Father, and of the Son, and of the Holy Spirit."

Father, look now with love upon your Church, and unseal for her the fountain of baptism.

By the power of the Spirit give to the water of this font the grace of your Son.

You created man in your own likeness: cleanse him from sin in a new birth to innocence by water and the Spirit.

The celebrant touches the water with his right hand and continues:
We ask you, Father, with your Son to send the Holy Spirit upon the water of this font. May all who are buried with Christ in the death of baptism rise also with him to newness of life. We ask this through Christ our Lord.

All:
Amen.

During the Easter season, if there is baptismal water which was consecrated at the Easter Vigil, the blessing and invocation of God over the water are nevertheless included, so that this theme of thanksgiving and petition may find a place in the baptism. The forms of this blessing and invocation are those found on pages 26–28, with the variations indicated at the end of each text.

RENUNCIATION OF SIN AND PROFESSION OF FAITH

The celebrant speaks to the parents and godparents in these words:

Dear parents and godparents: You have come here to present this child for baptism. By water and the Holy Spirit he (she) is to receive the gift of new life from God, who is love.

On your part, you must make it your constant care to bring him (her) up in the practice of the faith. See that the divine life which God gives him (her) is kept safe from the poison of sin, to grow always stronger in his (her) heart.

If your faith makes you ready to accept this responsibility, renew now the vows of your own baptism. Reject sin; profess your faith in Christ Jesus. This is the faith of the Church. This is the faith in which this child is about to be baptized.

The celebrant questions the parents and godparents.

A   Celebrant:

Do you reject Satan?

Parents and godparents:

I do.

Celebrant:

And all his works?

Parents and godparents:

I do.

Celebrant:

And all his empty promises?

Parents and godparents:

I do.

or:

B   Celebrant:

Do you reject sin, so as to live in the freedom of God's children?

Parents and godparents:

I do.

Celebrant:

Do you reject the glamor of evil, and refuse to be mastered by sin?

Parents and godparents:

I do.

Celebrant:

Do you reject Satan, father of sin and prince of darkness?

Parents and godparents:

I do.

According to circumstances, this second form may be expressed with greater precision by the conferences of bishops, especially in places where it is necessary for the parents and godparents to reject superstitious and magical practices used with children.

Next the celebrant asks for the threefold profession of faith from the parents and godparents:

Celebrant:

Do you believe in God, the Father almighty, creator of heaven and earth?

I do.

Celebrant:

Do you believe in Jesus Christ, his only Son, our Lord, who was born of the Virgin Mary, was crucified, died, and was buried, rose from the dead, and is now seated at the right hand of the Father?

Parents and godparents:

I do.

Celebrant:

Do you believe in the Holy Spirit, the holy catholic Church, the communion of saints, the forgiveness of sins, the resurrection of the body, and life everlasting?

Parents and godparents:

I do.

The celebrant and the congregation give their assent to this profession of faith:

Celebrant:

This is our faith. This is the faith of the Church. We are proud to profess it, in Christ Jesus our Lord.

All:

Amen.

If desired, some other formula may be used instead, or a suitable song by which the community expresses its faith with a single voice.

BAPTISM

The celebrant invites the family to the font and questions the parents and godparents:

Celebrant:

Is it your will that N. should be baptized in the faith of the Church, which we have all professed with you?

Parents and godparents:

It is.

He baptizes the child, saying:

N., I baptize you in the name of the Father,

He immerses the child or pours water upon it.

and of the Son,

He immerses the child or pours water upon it a second time.

and of the Holy Spirit.

He immerses the child or pours water upon it a third time.

After the child is baptized, it is appropriate for the people to sing a short acclamation:

This is the fountain of life,
water made holy by the suffering of Christ,
washing all the world.
You who are washed in this water
have hope of heaven's kingdom.

If the baptism is performed by the pouring of water, it is preferable that the child be held by the mother (or father). Where, however, it is felt that the existing custom should be retained, the godmother (or godfather) may hold the child. If baptism is by immersion, the mother or father (godmother or godfather) lifts the child out of the font.

EXPLANATORY RITES

ANOINTING AFTER BAPTISM

Then the celebrant says:

God the Father of our Lord Jesus Christ has freed you from sin, given you a new birth by water and the Holy Spirit, and welcomed you into his holy people. He now anoints you with the chrism of salvation. As Christ was anointed Priest, Prophet, and King, so may you live always as a member of his body, sharing everlasting life.

All:

Amen.

Then the celebrant anoints the child on the crown of the head with the sacred chrism, in silence.

CLOTHING WITH THE WHITE GARMENT

The celebrant says:

N., you have become a new creation, and have clothed yourself in Christ.

See in this white garment the outward sign of your Christian dignity. With your family and friends to help you by word and example, bring that dignity unstained into the everlasting life of heaven.

All:

Amen.

The white garment is put on the child. A different color is not permitted unless demanded by local custom. It is desirable that the family provide the garment.

LIGHTED CANDLE

The celebrant takes the Easter candle and says:

Receive the light of Christ.

Someone from the family (such as the father or godfather) lights the child's candle from the Easter candle.

The celebrant then says:

Parents and godparent (or: godparents), this light is entrusted to you to be kept burning brightly. This child of yours has been enlightened by Christ. He (she) is to walk always as a child of the light. May he (she) keep the flame of faith alive in his (her) heart. When the Lord comes, may he (she) go out to meet him with all the saints in the heavenly kingdom.

EPHPHETHA OR PRAYER OVER EARS AND MOUTH

If the conference of bishops decides to preserve the practice, the rite of *Ephphetha* follows. [In the United States it may be performed at the discretion of the minister.] The celebrant touches the ears and mouth of the child with his thumb, saying:

The Lord Jesus made the deaf hear and the dumb speak. May he soon touch your ears to receive his word, and your mouth to proclaim his faith, to the praise and glory of God the Father.

All:

Amen.

CONCLUSION OF THE RITE

Next there is a procession to the altar, unless the baptism was performed in the sanctuary. The lighted candle is carried for the child.

A baptismal song is appropriate at this time, e.g.:

You have put on Christ,
in him you have been baptized.
Alleluia, alleluia.

Other songs may be chosen.

The celebrant stands in front of the altar and addresses the parents, godparents, and the whole assembly in these or similar words:

Dearly beloved, this child has been reborn in baptism. He (she) is now called the child of God, for so indeed he (she) is. In confirmation he (she) will receive the fullness of God's Spirit. In holy communion he (she) will share the banquet of Christ's sacrifice, calling God his (her) Father in the midst of the Church. In the name of this child, in the Spirit of our common sonship, let us pray together in the words our Lord has given us:

All present join the celebrant in singing or saying:

Our Father,
who art in heaven,
hallowed be thy name;
thy kingdom come;
thy will be done on earth as it is in heaven.
Give us this day our daily bread;
and forgive us our trespasses
as we forgive those who trespass against us;
and lead us not into temptation,
but deliver us from evil.

BLESSING AND DISMISSAL

The celebrant first blesses the mother, who holds the child in her arms, then the father, and lastly the entire assembly:

Celebrant:

God the Father, through his Son, the Virgin Mary's child, has brought joy to all Christian mothers, as they see the hope of eternal life shine on their children. May he bless the mother of this child. She now thanks God for the gift of her child. May she be one with him (her) in thanking him for ever in heaven, in Christ Jesus our Lord.

All:

Amen.

Celebrant:

God is the giver of all life, human and divine. May he bless the father of this child. He and his wife will be the first teachers of their child in the ways of faith. May they be also the best of teachers, bearing witness to the faith by what they say and do, in Christ Jesus our Lord.

All:

Amen.

Celebrant:

By God's gift, through water and the Holy Spirit, we are reborn to everlasting life. In his goodness, may he continue to pour out his blessings upon these sons and daughters of his. May he make them always, wherever they may be, faithful members of his holy people. May he send his peace upon all who are gathered here, in Christ Jesus our Lord.

All:

Amen.

Celebrant:

May almighty God, the Father, and the Son, ✠ and the Holy Spirit, bless you.

All:

Amen.

Celebrant:

Go in peace.

All:

Thanks be to God.

For other forms of the blessing, see pages 35–37.

After the blessing, all may sing a hymn which suitably expresses thanksgiving and Easter joy, or they may sing the song of the Blessed Virgin Mary, the Magnificat.

Where there is the practice of bringing the baptized child to the altar of the Blessed Virgin Mary, this custom is observed if appropriate.

RITE OF BAPTISM
FOR SEVERAL CHILDREN

RECEPTION OF THE CHILDREN

If possible, baptism should take place on Sunday, the day on which the Church celebrates the paschal mystery. It should be conferred in a communal celebration for all the recently born children, and in the presence of the faithful, or at least of relatives, friends, and neighbors, who are all to take an active part in the rite.

It is the role of the father and mother, accompanied by the godparents, to present the child to the Church for baptism.

If there are very many children, and if there are several priests or deacons present, these may help the celebrant in the parts referred to below.

The people may sing a psalm or hymn suitable for the occasion. Meanwhile the celebrating priest or deacon, vested in alb or surplice, with a stole (with or without a cope) of festive color, and accompanied by the ministers, goes to the entrance of the church or to that part of the church where the parents and godparents are waiting with those who are to be baptized.

The celebrant greets all present, and especially the parents and godparents, reminding them briefly of the joy with which the parents welcomed their children as gifts from God, the source of life, who now wishes to bestow his own life on these little ones.

First the celebrant questions the parents of each child.

Celebrant:

What name do you give your child? (or: **have you given?**)

Parents:

N.

Celebrant:
What do you ask of God's Church for N.?

Parents:
Baptism.

The celebrant may choose other words for this dialogue.

The first reply may be given by someone other than the parents if local custom gives him the right to name the child.

In the second response the parents may use other words, e.g., faith or the grace of Christ or entrance into the Church or eternal life.

If there are many children to be baptized, the celebrant asks the names from all the parents together, and each family replies in turn. The second question may also be asked of all together.

Celebrant:
What name do you give each of these children? (or: have you given?)

Parents:
N., N., etc.

Celebrant:
What do you ask of God's Church for your children?

All:
Baptism.

The celebrant speaks to the parents in these or similar words:
You have asked to have your children baptized. In doing so you are accepting the responsibility of training them in the practice of the faith. It will be your duty to bring them up to keep God's commandments as Christ taught us, by loving God and our neighbor. Do you clearly understand what you are undertaking?

Parents:
We do.

This response is given by each family individually. But if there are many children to be baptized, the response may be given by all together.

Then the celebrant turns to the godparents and addresses them in these or similar words:

Are you ready to help these parents in their duty as Christian mothers and fathers?

All the godparents:

We are.

The celebrant continues:

N. and N. (or: **My dear children**), the Christian community welcomes you with great joy. In its name I claim you for Christ our Savior by the sign of his cross. I now trace the cross on your foreheads, and invite your parents (and godparents) to do the same.

He signs each child on the forehead, in silence. Then he invites the parents and, if it seems appropriate, the godparents to do the same.

The celebrant invites the parents, godparents, and the others to take part in the liturgy of the word. If circumstances permit, there is a procession to the place where this will be celebrated, during which a song is sung, e.g., Psalm 84:7, 8, 9ab:

Will you not give us life;
 and shall not your people rejoice in you?
Show us, O Lord, your kindness,
 and grant us your salvation.
I will hear what God proclaims;
 the Lord—for he proclaims peace to his people.

The children to be baptized may be carried to a separate place, where they remain until the end of the liturgy of the word.

LITURGY OF THE WORD

SCRIPTURAL READINGS AND HOMILY

One or even two gospel passages are read, during which all may sit if convenient.

Matthew 28:18-20

☩ A reading from the holy Gospel according to Matthew

Go, therefore, and make disciples of all nations, baptizing them in the name of the Father, and of the Son, and of the Holy Spirit.

Jesus said to the Eleven disciples:
"All power in heaven and on earth has been given to me.

Go, therefore, and make disciples of all nations,
   baptizing them in the name of the Father,
   and of the Son, and of the Holy Spirit,
   teaching them to observe all that I have commanded you.
And behold, I am with you always, until the end of the age."

The Gospel of the Lord.

Alternate choices of readings, together with responsorial psalms and verses before the gospel, are given on pages 39–56.

After the reading, the celebrant gives a short homily, explaining to those present the significance of what has been read. His purpose will be to lead them to a deeper understanding of the mystery of baptism and to encourage the parents and godparents to a ready acceptance of the responsibilities which arise from the sacrament.

After the homily, or in the course of or after the litany, it is desirable to have a period of silence while all pray at the invitation of the celebrant.

GENERAL INTERCESSIONS

Then the general intercessions are said:

Celebrant:

My brothers and sisters,* let us ask our Lord Jesus Christ to look lovingly on these children who are to be baptized, on their parents and godparents, and on all the baptized.

*At the discretion of the priest, other words which seem more suitable under the circumstances, such as friends, dearly beloved, brethren, may be used. This also applies to parallel instances in the liturgy.

Leader:

By the mystery of your death and resurrection, bathe these children in light, give them the new life of baptism and welcome them into your holy Church.

All:

Lord, hear our prayer.

Leader:

Through baptism and confirmation, make them your faithful followers and witnesses to your gospel.

All:

Lord, hear our prayer.

Leader:

Lead them by a holy life to the joys of God's kingdom.

All:

Lord, hear our prayer.

Leader:

Make the lives of their parents and godparents examples of faith to inspire these children.

All:

Lord, hear our prayer.

Leader:

Keep their families always in your love.

All:

Lord, hear our prayer.

Leader:

Renew the grace of our baptism in each one of us.

All:

Lord, hear our prayer.

Other forms may be chosen.

The celebrant next invites all present to invoke the saints. At this point, if the children have been taken out, they are brought back.

Holy Mary, Mother of God,	**pray for us.**
Saint John the Baptist,	**pray for us.**
Saint Joseph,	**pray for us.**
Saint Peter and Saint Paul,	**pray for us.**

The names of other saints may be added, especially the patrons of the children to be baptized, and of the church or locality. The litany concludes:

All holy men and women,	**pray for us.**

PRAYER OF EXORCISM AND ANOINTING BEFORE BAPTISM

After the invocations, the celebrant says:

A Almighty and ever-living God, you sent your only Son into the world to cast out the power of Satan, spirit of evil, to rescue man from the kingdom of darkness, and bring him into the splendor of your kingdom of light. We pray for these children: set them free from original sin, make them temples of your glory, and send your Holy Spirit to dwell within them. (We ask this) through Christ our Lord.

All:

Amen.

Another form of the prayer of exorcism

B Almighty God, you sent your only Son to rescue us from the slavery of sin, and to give us the freedom only your sons and daughters enjoy. We now pray for these children who will have to face the world with its temptations, and fight the devil in all his cunning. Your Son died and rose again to save us. By his victory over sin and death, cleanse these children from the stain of original sin. Strengthen them with the grace of Christ, and watch over them at every step in life's journey. (We ask this) through Christ our Lord.

All:

Amen.

The celebrant continues:

We anoint you with the oil of salvation in the name of Christ our Savior; may he strengthen you with his power, who lives and reigns for ever and ever.

All:

Amen.

He anoints each child on the breast with the oil of catechumens. If the number of children is large, the anointing may be done by several ministers.

If, for serious reasons, the conference of bishops so decides, the anointing before baptism may be omitted. [In the United States, it may be omitted only when the minister of baptism judges the omission to be pastorally necessary or desirable.] In that case the celebrant says once only:

May you have strength in the power of Christ our Savior, who lives and reigns for ever and ever.

All:

Amen.

And immediately he lays his hand on each child in silence.

If the baptistery is located outside the church or is not within view of the congregation, all go there in procession.

If the baptistery is located within view of the congregation, the celebrant, parents, and godparents go there with the children, while the others remain in their places.

If, however, the baptistery cannot accommodate the congregation, the baptism may be celebrated in a suitable place within the church, and the parents and godparents bring the child forward at the proper moment.

Meanwhile, if it can be done suitably, an appropriate song is sung, e.g., Psalm 23:

The LORD is my shepherd; I shall not want.
In verdant pastures he gives me repose;
Beside restful waters he leads me;
he refreshes my soul.
He guides me in right paths
for his name's sake.
Even though I walk in the dark valley
I fear no evil; for you are at my side
With your rod and your staff
that give me courage.
You spread the table before me
in the sight of my foes,
You anoint my head with oil;
my cup overflows.
Only goodness and kindness follow me
all the days of my life;
And I shall dwell in the house of the LORD
for years to come.

CELEBRATION OF THE SACRAMENT

When they come to the font, the celebrant briefly reminds the congregation of the wonderful work of God whose plan it is to sanctify man, body and soul, through water. He may use these or similar words:

A My dear brothers and sisters, we now ask God to give these children new life in abundance through water and the Holy Spirit.

or:

B My dear brothers and sisters, God uses the sacrament of water to give his divine life to those who believe in him. Let us turn to him, and ask him to pour his gift of life from this font on the children he has chosen.

BLESSING AND INVOCATION OF GOD OVER BAPTISMAL WATER

Then, turning to the font, he sings or says the following blessing (outside the Easter season):

A Father, you give us grace through sacramental signs, which tell us of the wonders of your unseen power.

In baptism we use your gift of water, which you have made a rich symbol of the grace you give us in this sacrament.

At the very dawn of creation your Spirit breathed on the waters, making them the wellspring of all holiness.

The waters of the great flood you made a sign of the waters of baptism, that make an end of sin and a new beginning of goodness.

Through the waters of the Red Sea you led Israel out of slavery, to be an image of God's holy people, set free from sin by baptism.

In the waters of the Jordan your Son was baptized by John and anointed with the Spirit.

Your Son willed that water and blood should flow from his side as he hung upon the cross.

After his resurrection he told his disciples: "Go out and teach all nations, baptizing them in the name of the Father, and of the Son, and of the Holy Spirit."

Father, look now with love upon your Church, and unseal for her the fountain of baptism.

25

By the power of the Spirit give to the water of this font the grace of your Son.

You created man in your own likeness: cleanse him from sin in a new birth to innocence by water and the Spirit.

The celebrant touches the water with his right hand and continues:
We ask you, Father, with your Son to send the Holy Spirit upon the water of this font. May all who are buried with Christ in the death of baptism rise also with him to newness of life. We ask this through Christ our Lord.

All:
Amen.

Other forms of the blessing:

B   Celebrant:
Praise to you, almighty God and Father, for you have created water to cleanse and to give life.

All:
Blessed be God (or some other suitable acclamation by the people).

Celebrant:
Praise to you, Lord Jesus Christ, the Father's only Son, for you offered yourself on the cross, that in the blood and water flowing from your side, and through your death and resurrection, the Church might be born.

All:
Blessed be God.

Celebrant:
Praise to you, God the Holy Spirit, for you anointed Christ at his baptism in the waters of Jordan, so that we might all be baptized into you.

All:
Blessed be God.

Celebrant:
*Come to us, Lord, Father of all, and make holy this water which you have created, so that all who are baptized in it may be washed clean of sin, and be born again to live as your children.

All:

Hear us, Lord (or some other suitable invocation).

Celebrant:

Make this water holy, Lord, so that all who are baptized into Christ's death and resurrection by this water may become more perfectly like your Son.

All:

Hear us, Lord.

The celebrant touches the water with his right hand and continues:

Lord, make holy this water which you have created, so that all those whom you have chosen may be born again by the power of the Holy Spirit, and may take their place among your holy people.

All:

Hear us, Lord.

*If the baptismal water has already been blessed the celebrant omits the invocation Come to us, Lord and those which follow it and says:

You have called your children, N., N., to this cleansing water that they may share in the faith of your Church and have eternal life. By the mystery of this consecrated water lead them to a new and spiritual birth. (We ask this) through Christ our Lord.

All:

Amen.

C   Celebrant:

Father, God of mercy, through these waters of baptism you have filled us with new life as your very own children.

All:

Blessed be God (or some other suitable acclamation by the people).

Celebrant:

From all who are baptized in water and the Holy Spirit, you have formed one people, united in your Son Jesus Christ.

All:

Blessed be God.

Celebrant:

You have set us free and filled our hearts with the Spirit of your love, that we may live in your peace.

All:

Blessed be God.

Celebrant:

You call those who have been baptized to announce the Good News of Jesus Christ to people everywhere.

All:

Blessed be God.

Celebrant:

*You have called your children, N., N., to this cleansing water and new birth that by sharing the faith of your Church they might have eternal life. Bless ✠ this water in which they will be baptized. We ask this in the name of Christ our Lord.

All:

Amen.

*If the baptismal water has already been blessed, the celebrant omits this last prayer and says:

You have called your children, N., N., to this cleansing water that they may share in the faith of your Church and have eternal life. By the mystery of this consecrated water lead them to a new and spiritual birth. (We ask this) through Christ our Lord.

All:

Amen.

During the Easter season, if there is baptismal water which was consecrated at the Easter Vigil, the blessing and invocation of God over the water are nevertheless included, so that this theme of thanksgiving and petition may find a place in the baptism. The forms of this blessing and invocation are those found in B and C above, with the variation indicated at the end of each text.

RENUNCIATION OF SIN AND PROFESSION OF FAITH

The celebrant speaks to the parents and godparents in these words: Dear parents and godparents: You have come here to present these children for baptism. By water and the Holy Spirit they are to receive the gift of new life from God, who is love.

On your part, you must make it your constant care to bring them up in the practice of the faith. See that the divine life which God gives them is kept safe from the poison of sin, to grow always stronger in their hearts.

If your faith makes you ready to accept this responsibility, renew now the vows of your own baptism. Reject sin; profess your faith in Christ Jesus. This is the faith of the Church. This is the faith in which these children are about to be baptized.

The celebrant questions the parents and godparents.

A   Celebrant:
Do you reject Satan?

Parents and godparents:
I do.

Celebrant:
And all his works?

Parents and godparents:
I do.

Celebrant:
And all his empty promises?

Parents and godparents:
I do.

or:

B   Celebrant:
Do you reject sin, so as to live in the freedom of God's children?

Parents and godparents:
I do.

Celebrant:
Do you reject the glamor of evil, and refuse to be mastered by sin?

Parents and godparents:
I do.

Celebrant:

Do you reject Satan, father of sin and prince of darkness?

Parents and godparents:

I do.

According to circumstances, this second form may be expressed with greater precision by the conferences of bishops, especially in places where it is necessary for the parents and godparents to reject superstitious and magical practices used with children.

Next the celebrant asks for the threefold profession of faith from the parents and godparents:

Celebrant:

Do you believe in God, the Father almighty, creator of heaven and earth?

Parents and godparents:

I do.

Celebrant:

Do you believe in Jesus Christ, his only Son, our Lord, who was born of the Virgin Mary, was crucified, died, and was buried, rose from the dead, and is now seated at the right hand of the Father?

Parents and godparents:

I do.

Celebrant:

Do you believe in the Holy Spirit, the holy catholic Church, the communion of saints, the forgiveness of sins, the resurrection of the body, and life everlasting?

Parents and godparents:

I do.

The celebrant and the congregation give their assent to this profession of faith:

Celebrant:

This is our faith. This is the faith of the Church. We are proud to profess it, in Christ Jesus our Lord.

All:

Amen.

If desired, some other formula may be used instead, or a suitable song by which the community expresses its faith with a single voice.

The celebrant invites the first of the families to the font. Using the name of the individual child, he questions the parents and godparents.

Celebrant:

Is it your will that N. should be baptized in the faith of the Church, which we have all professed with you?

Parents and godparents:

It is.

He baptizes the child, saying:

N., I baptize you in the name of the Father,

He immerses the child or pours water upon it.

and of the Son,

He immerses the child or pours water upon it a second time.

and of the Holy Spirit.

He immerses the child or pours water upon it a third time.

He asks the same question and performs the same action for each child.

After each baptism it is appropriate for the people to sing a short acclamation:

This is the fountain of life,
water made holy by the suffering of Christ,
washing all the world.
You who are washed in this water
have hope of heaven's kingdom.

If the baptism is performed by the pouring of water, it is preferable that the child be held by the mother (or father). Where, however, it is felt that the existing custom should be retained, the godmother (or godfather) may hold the child. If baptism is by immersion, the mother or father (godmother or godfather) lifts the child out of the font.

If the number of children to be baptized is large, and other priests or deacons are present, these may baptize some of the children in the way described above, and with the same form.

EXPLANATORY RITES

ANOINTING AFTER BAPTISM

Then the celebrant says:

God the Father of our Lord Jesus Christ has freed you from sin, given you a new birth by water and the Holy Spirit, and welcomed you into his holy people. He now anoints you with the chrism of salvation. As Christ was anointed Priest, Prophet, and King, so may you live always as members of his body, sharing everlasting life.

All:

Amen.

Next, the celebrant anoints each child on the crown of the head with chrism, in silence.

If the number of children is large and other priests or deacons are present, these may anoint some of the children with chrism.

CLOTHING WITH WHITE GARMENT

The celebrant says:

(N. and N.), you have become a new creation, and have clothed yourselves in Christ.

See in this white garment the outward sign of your Christian dignity. With your family and friends to help you by word and example, bring that dignity unstained into the everlasting life of heaven.

All:

Amen.

The white garments are put on the children. A different color is not permitted unless demanded by local custom. It is desirable that the families provide the garments.

LIGHTED CANDLE

The celebrant takes the Easter candle and says:

Receive the light of Christ.

Someone from each family (e.g., the father or godfather) lights the child's candle from the Easter candle.

The celebrant then says:

Parents and godparents, this light is entrusted to you to be kept burning brightly. These children of yours have been enlightened by Christ. They are to walk always as children of the light. May they keep the flame of faith alive in their hearts. When the Lord comes, may they go out to meet him with all the saints in the heavenly kingdom.

EPHPHETHA OR PRAYER OVER EARS AND MOUTH

If the conference of bishops decides to preserve the practice, the rite of *Ephphetha* follows. [In the United States it may be performed at the discretion of the minister.] The celebrant touches the ears and mouth of each child with his thumb, saying:

The Lord Jesus made the deaf hear and the dumb speak. May he soon touch your ears to receive his word, and your mouth to proclaim his faith, to the praise and glory of God the Father.

All:

Amen.

If the number of children is large, the celebrant says the formula once, but does not touch the ears and mouth.

CONCLUSION OF THE RITE

Next there is a procession to the altar, unless the baptism was performed in the sanctuary. The lighted candles are carried for the children.

A baptismal song is appropriate at this time, e.g.:

**You have put on Christ,
in him you have been baptized.
Alleluia, alleluia.**

Other songs may be chosen.

LORD'S PRAYER

Dearly beloved, these children have been reborn in baptism. They are now called children of God, for so indeed they are. In confirmation they will receive the fullness of God's Spirit. In holy communion they will share the banquet of Christ's sacrifice, calling God their Father in the midst of the Church. In their name, in the Spirit of our common sonship, let us pray together in the words our Lord has given us:

All present join the celebrant in singing or saying:

**Our Father,
who art in heaven,
hallowed be thy name;
thy kingdom come;
thy will be done on earth as it is in heaven.
Give us this day our daily bread;
and forgive us our trespasses
as we forgive those who trespass against us;
and lead us not into temptation,
but deliver us from evil.**

BLESSING AND DISMISSAL

The celebrant first blesses mothers, who hold the children in their arms, then the fathers, and lastly the entire assembly:

A Celebrant:

God the Father, through his Son, the Virgin Mary's child, has brought joy to all Christian mothers, as they see the hope of eternal life shine on their children. May he bless the mothers of these children. They now thank God for the gift of their children. May they be one with them in thanking him for ever in heaven, in Christ Jesus our Lord.

All:

Amen.

Celebrant:

God is the giver of all life, human and divine. May he bless the fathers of these children. With their wives they will be the first teachers of their children in the ways of faith. May they be also the best of teachers, bearing witness to the faith by what they say and do, in Christ Jesus our Lord.

All:

Amen.

Celebrant:

By God's gift, through water and the Holy Spirit, we are reborn to everlasting life. In his goodness, may he continue to pour out his blessings upon all present, who are his sons and daughters. May he make them always, wherever they may be, faithful members of his holy people. May he send his peace upon all who are gathered here, in Christ Jesus our Lord.

All:

Amen.

Celebrant:

May almighty God, the Father, and the Son, ✠ and the Holy Spirit, bless you.

All:

Amen.

Celebrant:

Go in peace.

All:

Thanks be to God.

Other forms of the final blessing:

B Celebrant:

May God the almighty Father, who filled the world with joy by giving us his only Son, bless these newly-baptized children. May they grow to be more fully like Jesus Christ our Lord.

All:

Amen.

Celebrant:

May almighty God, who gives life on earth and in heaven, bless the parents of these children. They thank him now for the gift he has given them. May they always show that gratitude in action by loving and caring for their children.

All:

Amen.

Celebrant:

May almighty God, who has given us a new birth by water and the Holy Spirit, generously bless all of us who are his faithful children. May we always live as his people, and may he bless all here present with his peace.

All:

Amen.

Celebrant:

May almighty God, the Father, and the Son, ✝ and the Holy Spirit, bless you.

All:

Amen.

Celebrant:

Go in peace.

All:

Thanks be to God.

C   Celebrant:

May God, the source of life and love, who fills the hearts of mothers with love for their children, bless the mothers of these newly-baptized children. As they thank God for a safe delivery, may they find joy in the love, growth, and holiness of their children.

All:

Amen.

Celebrant:

May God, the Father and model of all fathers, help these fathers to give good example, so that their children will grow to be mature Christians in all the fullness of Jesus Christ.

All:

Amen.

Celebrant:

May God, who loves all people, bless all the relatives and friends who are gathered here. In his mercy, may he guard them from evil and give them his abundant peace.

All:

Amen.

Celebrant:

And may almighty God, the Father, and the Son, ✠ and the Holy Spirit, bless you.

All:

Amen.

Celebrant:

Go in peace.

All:

Thanks be to God.

D Celebrant:

My brothers and sisters, we entrust you all to the mercy and help of God the almighty Father, his only Son, and the Holy Spirit. May he watch over your life, and may we all walk by the light of faith, and attain the good things he has promised us.

Go in peace, and may almighty God, the Father, and the Son, ✠ and the Holy Spirit, bless you.

All:

Amen.

After the blessing, all may sing a hymn which suitably expresses thanksgiving and Easter joy, or they may sing the song of the Blessed Virgin Mary, the Magnificat.

Where there is the practice of bringing baptized infants to the altar of the Blessed Virgin Mary, this custom is observed if appropriate.

OLD TESTAMENT READINGS

1   Exodus 17:3-7

A reading from the Book of Exodus

Give us water to drink (Exodus 17:2).

In their thirst for water,
   the people grumbled against Moses,
   saying, "Why did you ever make us leave Egypt?
Was it just to have us die here of thirst
   with our children and our livestock?"
So Moses cried out to the LORD,
   "What shall I do with this people?
A little more and they will stone me!"
The LORD answered Moses,
   "Go over there in front of the people,
   along with some of the elders of Israel,
   holding in your hand, as you go,
   the staff with which you struck the river.
I will be standing there in front of you on the rock
    in Horeb.
Strike the rock, and the water will flow from it
   for the people to drink."
This Moses did, in the presence of the elders of Israel.
The place was called Massah and Meribah,
   because the children of Israel quarreled there
   and tested the LORD, saying,
   "Is the LORD in our midst or not?"

The word of the Lord.

2   Ezekiel 36:24-28

A reading from the Book of the Prophet Ezekiel

I shall pour clean water upon you to cleanse you from all your impurities.

Thus says the Lord GOD:
I will take you away from among the nations,
   gather you from all the foreign lands,
   and bring you back to your own land.

I will sprinkle clean water upon you
     to cleanse you from all your impurities,
     and from all your idols I will cleanse you.
I will give you a new heart and place a new spirit within you,
     taking from your bodies your stony hearts
     and giving you natural hearts.
I will put my spirit within you and make you live by my
     statutes,
     careful to observe my decrees.
You shall live in the land I gave your fathers;
     you shall be my people, and I will be your God.

The word of the Lord.

3   Ezekiel 47:1-9, 12

A reading from the Book of the Prophet Ezekiel

*I saw water flowing from the temple, and all who were touched by it were
saved* (see *Roman Missal,* antiphon for blessing and sprinkling holy water
during the season of Easter).

The angel brought me, Ezekiel,
     back to the entrance of the temple of the Lord,
     and I saw water flowing out
     from beneath the threshold of the temple toward
          the east,
     for the façade of the temple was toward the east;
     the water flowed down from the right side of the
          temple,
     south of the altar.
He led me outside by the north gate,
     and around to the outer gate facing the east,
     where I saw water trickling from the right side.
Then when he had walked off to the east
     with a measuring cord in his hand,
     he measured off a thousand cubits
     and had me wade through the water,
     which was ankle-deep.

He measured off another thousand
and once more had me wade through the water,
which was now knee-deep.
Again he measured off a thousand and had me wade;
the water was up to my waist.
Once more he measured off a thousand,
but there was now a river through which I could
not wade;
for the water had risen so high it had become a river
that could not be crossed except by swimming.
He asked me, "Have you seen this, son of man?"
Then he brought me to the bank of the river, where he
had me sit.
Along the bank of the river I saw very many trees on
both sides.
He said to me,
"This water flows into the eastern district down
upon the Arabah,
and empties into the sea, the salt waters, which it
makes fresh.
Wherever the river flows,
every sort of living creature that can multiply shall live,
and there shall be abundant fish,
for wherever this water comes the sea shall be made fresh.
Along both banks of the river, fruit trees of every kind
shall grow;
their leaves shall not fade, nor their fruit fail.
Every month they shall bear fresh fruit,
for they shall be watered by the flow from the
sanctuary.
Their fruit shall serve for food, and their leaves for medicine."
The word of the Lord.

NEW TESTAMENT READINGS

1Romans 6:3-5

A reading from the Letter of Saint Paul to the Romans

Buried with him through baptism into death, we too might live in newness of life.

Brothers and sisters:
Are you unaware that we who were baptized into Christ Jesus
    were baptized into his death?
We were indeed buried with him through baptism into death,
    so that, just as Christ was raised from the dead
    by the glory of the Father,
    we too might live in newness of life.

For if we have grown into union with him through a death like
    his,
    we shall also be united with him in the resurrection.

The word of the Lord.

2Romans 8:28-32

A reading from the Letter of Saint Paul to the Romans

To be conformed to the image of his Son.

Brothers and sisters:
    We know that all things work for good for those who love
        God,
    who are called according to his purpose.
For those he foreknew he also predestined
    to be conformed to the image of his Son,
    so that he might be the firstborn
    among many brothers.
And those he predestined he also called;
    and those he called he also justified;
    and those he justified he also glorified.

What then shall we say to this?
If God is for us, who can be against us?

He who did not spare his own Son
  but handed him over for us all,
  how will he not also give us everything else along
    with him?

The word of the Lord.

3

A reading from the first Letter of Saint Paul to the Corinthians

For in one Spirit we were all baptized into one Body.

Brothers and sisters:
As a body is one though it has many parts,
  and all the parts of the body, though many, are
    one body,
  so also Christ.
For in one Spirit we were all baptized into one Body,
  whether Jews or Greeks, slaves or free persons,
  and we were all given to drink of one Spirit.

The word of the Lord.

4

A reading from the Letter of Saint Paul to the Galatians

*All of you who were baptized into Christ have clothed yourselves
with Christ.*

Brothers and sisters:
Through faith you are all children of God in Christ Jesus.
For all of you who were baptized into Christ
  have clothed yourselves with Christ.
There is neither Jew nor Greek,
  there is neither slave nor free person,
  there is not male and female;
  for you are all one in Christ Jesus.

The word of the Lord.

5

A reading from the Letter of Saint Paul to the Ephesians

There is one Lord, one faith, one baptism.

Brothers and sisters:
I, a prisoner for the Lord,
  urge you to live in a manner worthy of the call you have
    received,
  with all humility and gentleness, with patience,
  bearing with one another through love,
  striving to preserve the unity of the spirit
  through the bond of peace:
  one Body and one Spirit,
  as you were also called to the one hope of your call;
  one Lord, one faith, one baptism;
  one God and Father of all,
  who is over all and through all and in all.

The word of the Lord.

6

A reading from the first Letter of Saint Peter

You are a chosen race, a royal priesthood.

Beloved:
Come to the Lord, a living stone, rejected by human beings
  but chosen and precious in the sight of God,
  and, like living stones,
  let yourselves be built into a spiritual house
  to be a holy priesthood to offer spiritual sacrifices
    acceptable to God through Jesus Christ.

You are *a chosen race, a royal priesthood,*
  a holy nation, a people of his own,
  so that you may announce the praises of him
  who called you out of darkness into his wonderful light.

Once you were *no people*
  but now you are God's people;
you *had not received mercy*
  but now you have received mercy.

The word of the Lord.

RESPONSORIAL PSALMS

1   Psalm 23:1-3a, 3b-4, 5, 6

℞. (1) **The Lord is my shepherd; there is nothing I shall want.**

The LORD is my shepherd; I shall not want.
    In verdant pastures he gives me repose;
Beside restful waters he leads me;
    he refreshes my soul.

℞. **The Lord is my shepherd; there is nothing I shall want.**

He guides me in right paths
    for his name's sake.
Even though I walk in the dark valley
    I fear no evil; for you are at my side
With your rod and your staff
    that give me courage.

℞. **The Lord is my shepherd; there is nothing I shall want.**

You spread the table before me
    in the sight of my foes;
You anoint my head with oil;
    my cup overflows.

℞. **The Lord is my shepherd; there is nothing I shall want.**

Only goodness and kindness follow me
    all the days of my life;
And I shall dwell in the house of the Lord
    for years to come.

℞. **The Lord is my shepherd; there is nothing I shall want.**

2   Psalm 27:1bcde, 4, 8b-9abc, 13-14

℞. (1b) **The Lord is my light and my salvation.**
or: (Ephesians 5:14) **Wake up and rise from death: Christ will
    shine upon you!**

The LORD is my light and my salvation;
    whom should I fear?
The LORD is my life's refuge;
    of whom should I be afraid?

℟. **The Lord is my light and my salvation.**
or: **Wake up and rise from death: Christ will shine upon you!**

One thing I ask of the Lord;
   this I seek:
To dwell in the house of the LORD
   all the days of my life,
That I may gaze on the loveliness of the LORD
   and contemplate his temple.

℟. **The Lord is my light and my salvation.**
or: **Wake up and rise from death: Christ will shine upon you!**

Your presence, O LORD, I seek.
Hide not your face from me;
   do not in anger repel your servant.
You are my helper: cast me not off.

℟. **The Lord is my light and my salvation.**
or: **Wake up and rise from death: Christ will shine upon you!**

I believe that I shall see the bounty of the LORD
   in the land of the living.
Wait for the LORD with courage;
   be stouthearted, and wait for the LORD.

℟. **The Lord is my light and my salvation.**
or: **Wake up and rise from death: Christ will shine upon you!**

3   Psalm 34:2-3, 6-7, 8-9, 14-15, 16-17, 18-19

℟. (6a) **Look to him, that you may be radiant with joy!**
or: (9a) **Taste and see the goodness of the Lord.**

I will bless the LORD at all times;
   his praise shall ever be in my mouth.
Let my soul glory in the LORD;
   the lowly will hear me and be glad.

℟. **Look to him, that you may be radiant with joy!**
or: **Taste and see the goodness of the Lord.**

Look to him that you may be radiant with joy,
   and your faces may not blush with shame.
When the poor one called out, the LORD heard,
   and from all his distress he saved him.

R7. **Look to him, that you may be radiant with joy!**
or: **Taste and see the goodness of the Lord.**

The angel of the LORD encamps
   around those who fear him, and delivers them.
Taste and see how good the LORD is;
   blessed the man who takes refuge in him.

R7. **Look to him, that you may be radiant with joy!**
or: **Taste and see the goodness of the Lord.**

Keep your tongue from evil,
   your lips from speaking guile;
Turn from evil, and do good;
   seek peace, and follow after it.

R7. **Look to him, that you may be radiant with joy!**
or: **Taste and see the goodness of the Lord.**

The LORD has eyes for the just
   and ears for their cry.
The LORD confronts the evildoers,
   to destroy remembrance of them from the earth.

R7. **Look to him, that you may be radiant with joy!**
or: **Taste and see the goodness of the Lord.**

When the just cry out, the LORD hears them,
   and from all their distress he rescues them.
The LORD is close to the brokenhearted,
   and those who are crushed in spirit he saves.

R7. **Look to him, that you may be radiant with joy!**
or: **Taste and see the goodness of the Lord.**

ALLELUIA VERSE AND VERSE BEFORE THE GOSPEL

Outside of Lent, the cantor sings Alleluia; it is then repeated by the people. The cantor then sings one of the verses given below, and the people repeat Alleluia.

During Lent, the same pattern is followed, except that one of the following invocations replaces the Alleluia:

(a) Praise to you, Lord Jesus Christ, king of endless glory!
(b) Praise and honor to you, Lord Jesus Christ!
(c) Glory and praise to you, Lord Jesus Christ!
(d) Glory to you, Word of God, Lord Jesus Christ!

1   John 3:16

**God so loved the world that he gave his only-begotten Son,
so that everyone who believes in him might have eternal
  life.**

2   John 8:12

**I am the light of the world, says the Lord;
whoever follows me will have the light of life.**

3   John 14:6

**I am the way and the truth and the life, says the Lord;
no one comes to the Father, except through me.**

4   Ephesians 4:5-6a

**There is one Lord, one faith, one baptism,
one God and the Father of all.**

5   See 2 Timothy 1:10

**Our Savior Jesus Christ has destroyed death
and brought life to light through the Gospel.**

6   1 Peter 2:9

**You are a chosen race, a royal priesthood, a holy nation:
announce the praises of him who called you
out of darkness into his wonderful light.**

GOSPEL

1 Matthew 22:35-40

✝ A reading from the holy Gospel according to Matthew

This is the greatest and the first commandment.

One of the Pharisees, a scholar of the law, tested Jesus by
    asking,
    "Teacher, which commandment in the law is the greatest?"
He said to him,
    "You shall love the Lord, your God, with all your heart,
    with all your soul, and with all your mind.
This is the greatest and the first commandment.
The second is like it:
    You shall love your neighbor as yourself.
The whole law and the prophets depend on these two
    commandments."

The Gospel of the Lord.

2 Matthew 28:18-20

✝ A reading from the holy Gospel according to Matthew

*Go, therefore, and make disciples of all nations, baptizing them in the
name of the Father, and of the Son, and of the Holy Spirit.*

Jesus said to the Eleven disciples:
"All power in heaven and on earth has been given to me.
Go, therefore, and make disciples of all nations,
    baptizing them in the name of the Father,
    and of the Son, and of the Holy Spirit,
    teaching them to observe all that I have commanded you.
And behold, I am with you always, until the end of
    the age."

The Gospel of the Lord.

3   Mark 1:9-11

☩ **A reading from the holy Gospel according to Mark**

Jesus was baptized in the Jordan by John.

Jesus came from Nazareth of Galilee
   and was baptized in the Jordan by John.
On coming up out of the water he saw the heavens being torn
      open
   and the Spirit, like a dove, descending upon him.
And a voice came from the heavens,
   "You are my beloved Son; with you I am well pleased."

The Gospel of the Lord.

4   Mark 10:13-16

☩ **A reading from the holy Gospel according to Mark**

Let the children come to me; do not prevent them.

People were bringing children to Jesus that he might touch
      them,
   but the disciples rebuked them.
When Jesus saw this he became indignant and said to them,
   "Let the children come to me; do not prevent them,
   for the Kingdom of God belongs to such as these.
Amen, I say to you,
   whoever does not accept the Kingdom of God like a child
   will not enter it."
Then he embraced them and blessed them,
   placing his hands on them.

The Gospel of the Lord.

5   Mark 12:28-34 *or* 12:28-31

☩ **A reading from the holy Gospel according to Mark**

Hear O Israel! You shall love the Lord, your God, with all your heart.

LONG FORM

One of the scribes came to Jesus and asked him,
   "Which is the first of all the commandments?"

Jesus replied, "The first is this:
Hear, O Israel!
The Lord our God is Lord alone!
You shall love the Lord your God with all your heart,
with all your soul, with all your mind,
and with all your strength.
The second is this:
You shall love your neighbor as yourself.
There is no other commandment greater than these."
The scribe said to him,
"Well said, teacher. You are right in saying,
'He is One and there is no other than he.'
And 'to love him with all your heart,
with all your understanding,
with all your strength,
and to love your neighbor as yourself'
is worth more than all burnt offerings and sacrifices."
And when Jesus saw that he answered with
understanding,
he said to him,
"You are not far from the Kingdom of God."
And no one dared to ask him any more questions.

⌐ The Gospel of the Lord.

or:

SHORT FORM

One of the scribes came to Jesus and asked him,
"Which is the first of all the commandments?"
Jesus replied, "The first is this:
'Hear, O Israel! The Lord our God is Lord alone!
You shall love the Lord your God with all your heart,
with all your soul, with all your mind,
and with all your strength.'
The second is this:
'You shall love your neighbor as yourself.'
There is no other commandment greater than these."

⌐ The Gospel of the Lord.

✠ A reading from the holy Gospel according to John

No one can see the Kingdom of God without being born from above.

There was a Pharisee named Nicodemus, a ruler of
the Jews.
He came to Jesus at night and said to him,
"Rabbi, we know that you are a teacher who has come
from God,
for no one can do these signs that you are doing
unless God is with him."
Jesus answered and said to him,
"Amen, amen, I say to you,
unless one is born from above,
he cannot see the Kingdom of God."
Nicodemus said to him,
"How can a man once grown old be born again?
Surely he cannot reenter his mother's womb and be born
again, can he?"
Jesus answered,
"Amen, amen, I say to you,
unless one is born of water and Spirit
he cannot enter the Kingdom of God.
What is born of flesh is flesh
and what is born of spirit is spirit."

The Gospel of the Lord.

✠ A reading from the holy Gospel according to John

A spring of water welling up to eternal life.

Jesus came to a town of Samaria called Sychar,
near the plot of land that Jacob had given to his
son Joseph.
Jacob's well was there.
Jesus, tired from his journey, sat down there at
the well.
It was about noon.

A woman of Samaria came to draw water.
Jesus said to her,
  "Give me a drink."
His disciples had gone into the town to buy food.
The Samaritan woman said to him,
  "How can you, a Jew, ask me, a Samaritan woman, for a
    drink?"
—For Jews use nothing in common with Samaritans.—
Jesus answered and said to her,
  "If you knew the gift of God
  and who is saying to you, 'Give me a drink,'
  you would have asked him
  and he would have given you living water."
The woman said to him,
  "Sir, you do not even have a bucket and the cistern is deep;
  where then can you get this living water?
Are you greater than our father Jacob,
  who gave us this cistern and drank from it himself
  with his children and his flocks?"
Jesus answered and said to her,
  "Everyone who drinks this water will be thirsty again;
  but whoever drinks the water I shall give will never thirst;
  the water I shall give will become in him
  a spring of water welling up to eternal life."

The Gospel of the Lord.

8

John 6:44-47

✠ A reading from the holy Gospel according to John

Whoever believes has eternal life.

Jesus said to the crowds:
"No one can come to me unless the Father who sent
    me draw him,
  and I shall raise him on the last day.
It is written in the prophets:

  They shall all be taught by God.

Everyone who listens to my Father and learns from him comes
    to me.

Not that anyone has seen the Father
    except the one who is from God;
    he has seen the Father.
Amen, amen, I say to you,
    whoever believes has eternal life."

The Gospel of the Lord.

9   John 7:37b-39a

✝ A reading from the holy Gospel according to John

Rivers of living water will flow.

Jesus stood up and exclaimed,
    "Let anyone who thirsts come to me and drink.
Whoever believes in me, as Scripture says:

    Rivers of living water will flow from within him."

He said this in reference to the Spirit
    that those who came to believe in him were
        to receive.

The Gospel of the Lord.

10   John 9:1-7

✝ A reading from the holy Gospel according to John

So he went and washed and came back able to see.

As Jesus passed by he saw a man blind from birth.
His disciples asked him,
    "Rabbi, who sinned, this man or his parents,
    that he was born blind?"
Jesus answered,
    "Neither he nor his parents sinned;
    it is so that the works of God might be made visible through
        him.
We have to do the works of the one who sent me while it is day.
Night is coming when no one can work.
While I am in the world, I am the light of the world."

When he had said this, he spat on the ground
  and made clay with the saliva,
  and smeared the clay on his eyes, and said to him,
  "Go wash in the Pool of Siloam" (which means Sent).
So he went and washed, and came back able to see.

The Gospel of the Lord.

11

✛ A reading from the holy Gospel according to John

Whoever remains in me and I in him will bear much fruit.

Jesus said to his disciples:
"I am the true vine, and my Father is the vine grower.
He takes away every branch in me that does not
    bear fruit,
  and everyone that does he prunes so that it bears more fruit.
You are already pruned because of the word that I spoke to
    you.
Remain in me, as I remain in you.
Just as a branch cannot bear fruit on its own
  unless it remains on the vine,
  so neither can you unless you remain in me.
I am the vine, you are the branches.
Whoever remains in me and I in him will bear
    much fruit,
  because without me you can do nothing.
Anyone who does not remain in me
  will be thrown out like a branch and wither;
  people will gather them and throw them into a fire
  and they will be burned.
If you remain in me and my words remain in you,
  ask for whatever you want and it will be done for you.
By this is my Father glorified,
  that you bear much fruit and become my disciples.
As the Father loves me, so I also love you.
Remain in my love.

If you keep my commandments, you will remain in
    my love,
    just as I have kept my Father's commandments
    and remain in his love.

"I have told you this so that my joy may be in you
    and your joy may be complete."

The Gospel of the Lord.

12

✠ A reading from the holy Gospel according to John

*One soldier thrust his lance into his side, and immediately Blood and water
flowed out.*

Since it was preparation day,
    in order that the bodies might not remain on the cross on
      the sabbath,
    for the sabbath day of that week was a solemn one,
    the Jews asked Pilate that their legs be broken
    and they be taken down.
So the soldiers came and broke the legs of the first
    and then of the other one who was crucified with Jesus.
But when they came to Jesus and saw that he was
    already dead,
    they did not break his legs,
    but one soldier thrust his lance into his side,
    and immediately Blood and water flowed out.
An eyewitness has testified, and his testimony is true;
    he knows that he is speaking the truth,
    so that you also may come to believe.

The Gospel of the Lord.